LEGACIES
SPORTS AND ENTERTAINMENT

Peter Hicks

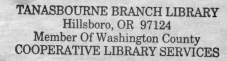
Thomson Learning • New York

Legacies

Architecture
Sports and Entertainment

Cover picture: More than 3,500 years ago, the Egyptians sailed on the Nile River with boats made of wood, like the one in the center. Today, water is still vital for both trade and outdoor pursuits, such as windsurfing.

First published in the
United States in 1995 by
Thomson Learning
115 Fifth Avenue
New York, NY 10003

First published in Great Britain in 1994 by Wayland (Publishers) Ltd.

Library of Congress Cataloging-in-Publication Data
Hicks, Peter.
  Sports and entertainment/ Peter Hicks.
    p.   cm.—(Legacies)
  "First published in Great Britain in 1994 by Wayland (Publishers) Ltd."—T.p. verso.
  Includes bibliographical references and index.
  ISBN 1-56847-245-5 2190 4834 7/99
    1. Recreation—History—Juvenile literature. 2. Sports—History—Juvenile literature.
  3. History, Ancient—Juvenile literature. [1. Recreation—History. 2. Sports—History.
  3. History, Ancient.] I. Title. II. Series: Legacies (New York, N.Y.)
  GV17.H53   1995
  1995—dc20   95-35339

Printed in Italy

Contents

A legacy is something handed down from an ancestor or predecessor. The modern world has inherited many different legacies from ancient civilizations. This book explores the sports and entertainment legacies of the ancient world.

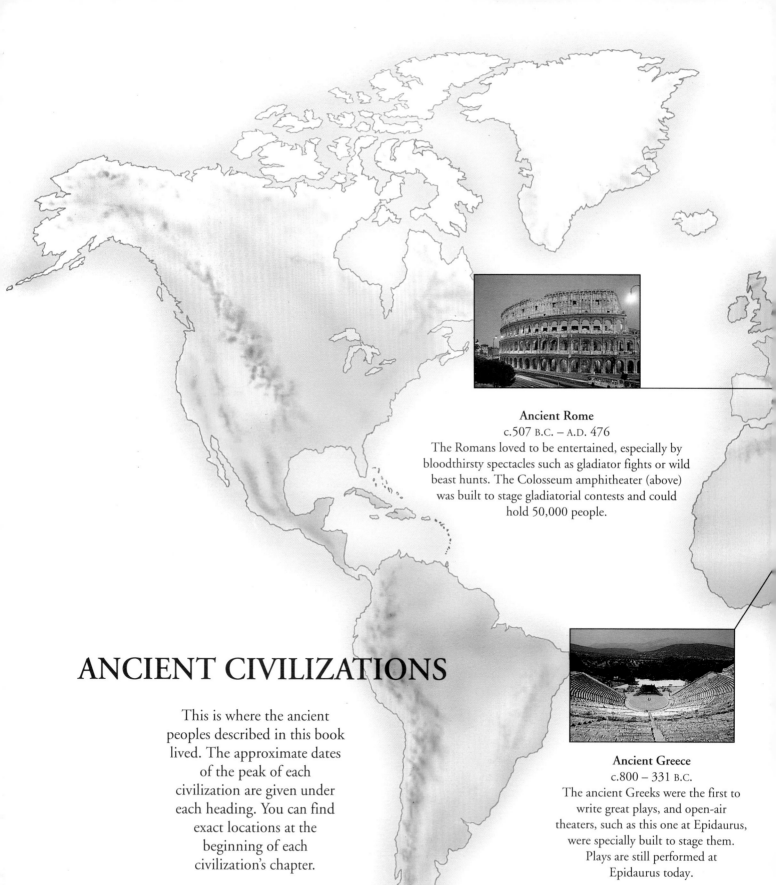

ANCIENT CIVILIZATIONS

This is where the ancient peoples described in this book lived. The approximate dates of the peak of each civilization are given under each heading. You can find exact locations at the beginning of each civilization's chapter.

Ancient Rome
c.507 B.C. – A.D. 476
The Romans loved to be entertained, especially by bloodthirsty spectacles such as gladiator fights or wild beast hunts. The Colosseum amphitheater (above) was built to stage gladiatorial contests and could hold 50,000 people.

Ancient Greece
c.800 – 331 B.C.
The ancient Greeks were the first to write great plays, and open-air theaters, such as this one at Epidaurus, were specially built to stage them. Plays are still performed at Epidaurus today.

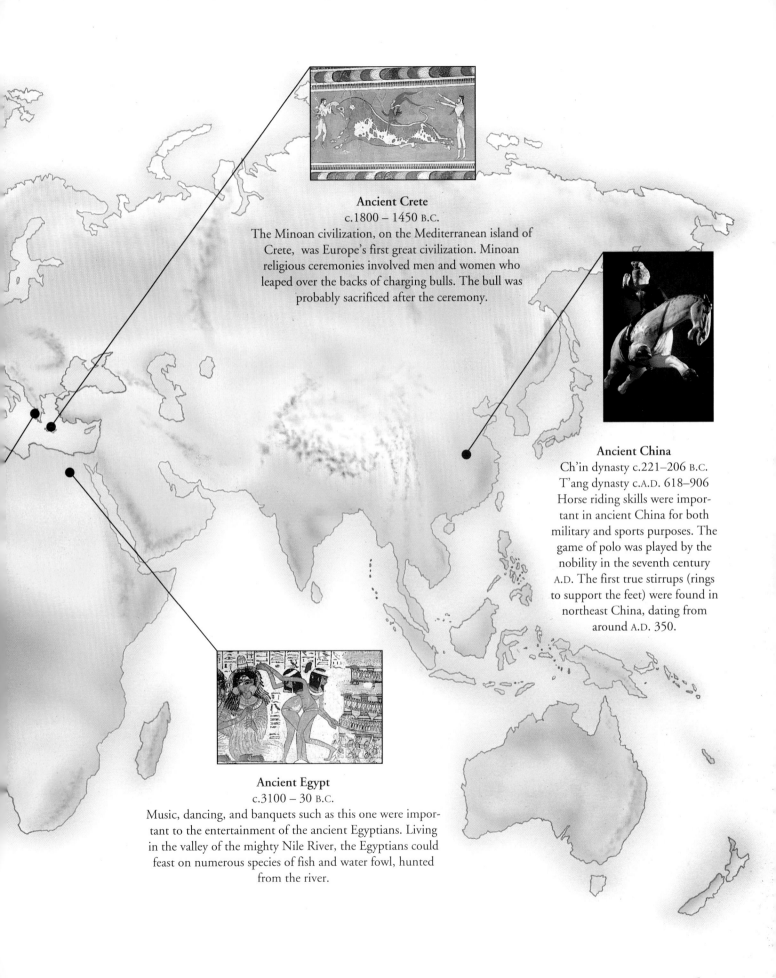

Ancient Crete
c.1800 – 1450 B.C.
The Minoan civilization, on the Mediterranean island of Crete, was Europe's first great civilization. Minoan religious ceremonies involved men and women who leaped over the backs of charging bulls. The bull was probably sacrificed after the ceremony.

Ancient China
Ch'in dynasty c.221–206 B.C.
T'ang dynasty c.A.D. 618–906
Horse riding skills were important in ancient China for both military and sports purposes. The game of polo was played by the nobility in the seventh century A.D. The first true stirrups (rings to support the feet) were found in northeast China, dating from around A.D. 350.

Ancient Egypt
c.3100 – 30 B.C.
Music, dancing, and banquets such as this one were important to the entertainment of the ancient Egyptians. Living in the valley of the mighty Nile River, the Egyptians could feast on numerous species of fish and water fowl, hunted from the river.

chapter one

ENTERTAINMENT: MODERN AND ANCIENT

▼ *The University of Michigan Stadium is packed with spectators watching a football game. Although we live in an age of mass-spectator sports, this scene would have been familiar to the ancient Greeks and Romans.*

Entertainment is an important way of relieving the stresses of modern life. People in developed countries have more leisure time now than at any time in history. What people do in this time is very important, be it hi-tech home-based entertainment such as watching television or videotapes, playing computer games, going to a movie, or going to see spectator sports such as baseball, football, or basketball. These are all popular ways of relaxing.

It wasn't much different in the past. In ancient times, the struggle against starvation made life and work hard, so any entertainment was a popular diversion. The rich, who were rulers, landowners, or merchants, tended to have more leisure time and more access to entertainment. However, poorer people who lived in or near a town or city could see regular entertainments. Many ancient entertainments were similar to the hard and brutish life that some people lived. Many involved cruelty to other human beings and animals. Other sports involved running, jumping, chasing, throwing, aiming, and prey-killing, which used hunting skills known since the Stone Age. These skills are features of many modern team games and blood sports today. Many entertainments that we take for granted today have their roots in ancient civilizations. Their legacies have left a mark in the sports and cultural entertainments of the modern era.

▼ *This is the original stadium at Olympia in Greece, as it is today. The stadium is one "stadion" long (607 feet), which is where the word "stadium" comes from. There were no seats for spectators, and the athletes entered the stadium through a tunnel off the bottom left of the picture. You can see the starting line and judges' box halfway down on the right.*

Every four years, millions of viewers all over the world watch the Olympic Games on television. Although there are many new sports in the modern Olympics, athletics, boxing, and wrestling date back to the original Olympic Games, held in Greece in 776 B.C. The Olympic Games were held every four years, as they are now. Dedicated to the god Zeus, they were taken very seriously. If any Greek states were at war with each other, the fighting had to stop so that their athletes could attend the five-day Games. The first modern Olympics were held in Athens in 1896, and were the idea of a Frenchman, Pierre de Coubertin. He wanted friendship to develop among young people from all over the world. He also wanted people to take part for the glory of winning and not for prizes or money. However, our modern Olympics have been criticized for drug scandals, political intrigue, and money payments. We shall find out if the ancient Olympics were any different.

▼ *The ancient Greek theater at Epidaurus has been restored. It was built to hold 16,000 spectators and, despite its size, even the people in the top row can hear sound clearly. The word "theater" comes from the Greek word "theatron," meaning "seeing place."*

◄ The layout of modern theaters and concert halls is very similar to that of ancient Greek theaters, such as Epidaurus. The tiered rows of seats, raised one above the other, mean that as many people as possible can see the stage. This is the Symphony Hall of the Birmingham International Conference Centre in England, which was built in 1992. The theater seats 2,200 people.

Nowadays, there are theaters all over the world. Even in an age of television, visiting theaters to see plays is still very popular. Over 2,500 years ago, Greek theater thrived. Ancient Greek theater originated from a festival for the wine god, Dionysus. Singers and dancers, called a "chorus," performed excerpts taken from the life of Dionysus. Ancient Greek plays are often performed today, and we use Greek names for places in modern theaters, such as the "orchestra" (from the Greek word meaning "to dance"), which was and still is the place where the musicians and chorus performed.

chapter two

ANCIENT
CRETE

Between 2800 and 1150 B.C., the ancient Minoan civilization grew and prospered on the island of Crete in the Mediterranean. It is called Minoan after one of its legendary kings, King Minos. King Minos figures in a famous legend about a monster, called a minotaur, who was half man and half bull. In the legend, the minotaur lived in a maze, or labyrinth, and each year ate fourteen young men and women from Athens. This was an offering to Crete from the city of Athens in Greece for losing an earlier war. When Theseus, son of the king of Athens, became one of the fourteen, he entered the labyrinth and finally killed the minotaur.

▼ *This fresco shows the Minoan sport of bull leaping. To complete these leaps would take the agility of an Olympic gymnast together with the balance of a bareback rider!*

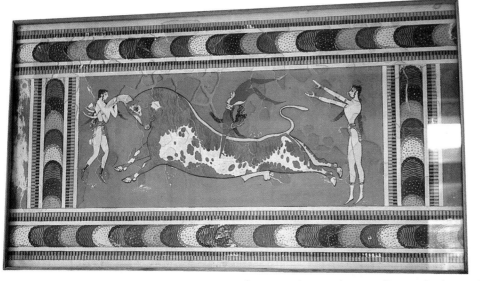

This story is a myth, but the bull was central to Minoan entertainment, respected for its strength, size, and fertility. It was used in a daring and deadly game called bull leaping. Wall paintings called frescos have been found that show young men and women leaping and somersaulting over running bulls. It is believed that the athletes first grabbed the bull's horns, hoisted themselves above and through them, somersaulted, landed, and bounced off the bull's back. Bull leaping was an

◀ Bull riding in the rodeo is so dangerous for the rider that brightly dressed clowns are ready to distract the bull in case the rider falls. This clown is having trouble keeping out of the bull's way!

extremely dangerous sport and the athletes risked a serious injury. Minoans also lassoed and wrestled bulls to the ground by their horns, just as cowboys and cowgirls do in the American rodeo today.

In the modern world, the bull is the center of both Spanish bullfighting and the American rodeo. In Spanish bullfighting, men called banderillos and picadors wound the bull with banderillas (short, barbed, colored staves) and lances until it is weak. Then the matador – the bullfighter – dodges the bull's charges while trying to kill it with a sword. Before the fight begins, clowns perform acrobatic skills similar to those performed in Minoan bull leaping, somersaulting, and cartwheeling in the arena to entertain the audience. In the rodeo, the most dangerous event is bull riding. The riders, who can be men or women, have to stay on a jumping, twisting, kicking bull for eight seconds. These modern riders, like the ancient Minoans, have to combine strength and agility with courage.

▼ During the July festival of San Fermin in Pamplona, Spain, hundreds of bulls are let loose through the town. Young men wearing red neckerchiefs are chased down the streets to the bull ring. Other spectators have to scramble out of the way.

BOXING

The Minoan civilization has the earliest references to boxing. Modern boxing, which is also an Olympic sport, is beamed to millions of television screens all over the world. Many fights are long, bruising, and violent exchanges, and boxers sometimes get seriously hurt or even killed. Doctors have to be in attendance, and referees are supposed to stop the fight if one of the boxers has taken too much punishment.

▶ *This Minoan fresco from the sixteenth century B.C. shows two children boxing. We are not sure of the rules, but it is likely that slaps as well as punches were used.*

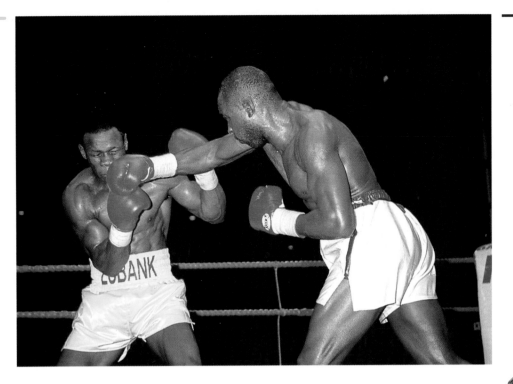

◀ *Despite its brutality, modern world championship boxing is very popular with both spectators and gamblers.*

▼ *The* Boxer of Apollonius *is a later Greek bronze. You can see the protective leather thongs around his wrists and hands.*

Minoan boxers can be seen on ancient frescos and vases, wearing helmets like the leather helmets that modern boxers wear in some matches. Some Minoan boxers wore their hair loose in curls hanging down their backs. Like boxers today, Minoan boxers wore calf-high boots to strengthen their ankles while they ducked and weaved around their opponent. Around the midriff they wore loincloths or short kilts. To protect their fingers and knuckles, modern boxers have them taped together before putting on their boxing gloves. Minoan boxers also protected their fists by wearing leather thongs over them that strengthened their punches. They may have worn brass knuckles: metal guards slipped over the fingers to increase the damage of a punch. The bronze helmets some boxers wore might well have been necessary.

chapter three

ANCIENT EGYPT

Six thousand years ago, ancient Egypt was a highly developed civilization. It thrived until 30 B.C., when it was taken over by the Roman Empire. The mighty Nile River, which flows through Egypt, was known as the "River of Life" because it brought great fertility to the river valley each year by leaving rich deposits of silt. Ancient Egyptian art, which decorated the insides of tombs and temples, shows that the Nile River was central to many forms of recreation in or on the water.

Mediterranean Sea

Nile Delta

Nile River

EGYPT

KEY
Area of fertile floodplain

▶ In ancient Egypt, big boats were made of wood held together with wooden pegs and ropes. Smaller boats, like those on page 17, were made of bundles of reeds tied together.

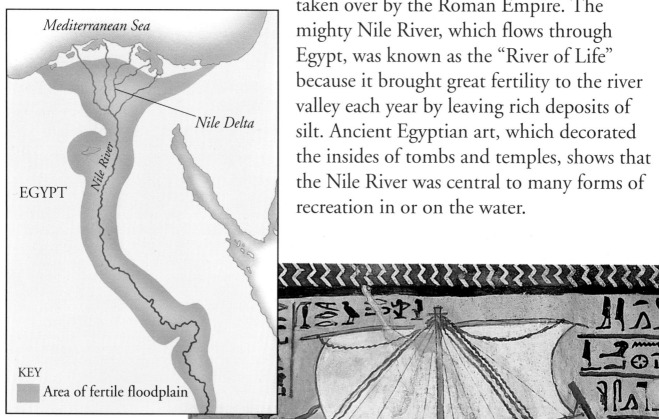

Today, water sports are a major form of entertainment. On the world's seas, rivers, and lakes, you can often see swimmers, sailors, water-skiers, parasailors, jet-skiers, surfers, and windsurfers. Some people enjoy competing, while others enjoy water sports just for fun. Many people choose beach vacations with a warm climate because of the attraction of water sports.

▲ *Today, windsurfing is one of many sports that make use of water for enjoyment. You can windsurf all over the world, on lakes or on the sea, as long as there is a good wind blowing.*

In ancient Egypt, many activities took place on the river, including sailing, trade, and fishing. Being able to swim was a good idea in case there was an accident, but Egyptians also swam for pleasure. Wall paintings show women swimming under water to catch waterfowl, and a form of crawl was taught. The crawl, so different from the more natural dog paddle style of swimming, is now the fastest swimming style. Swimming lessons were compulsory for the households of Egyptian royalty and nobility. An ancient document tells how a nobleman was instructed by the Pharaoh "to take swimming lessons along with the royal children."

The Egyptians were excellent boatbuilders, often using reeds, which grew in great abundance along the Nile, as their main building material. These boats were used in both work and play. Tomb frescos show young men in boats, armed with long poles, trying to push each other into the water. They also tried to tip their opponents' boat over. These games are very similar to competitions held today between lumberjacks in the Canadian logging games.

Rowing
Rowing was a popular water sport. The pharaohs celebrated with rowing festivals. At one, the pharaoh Amenophis II beat 200 other oarsmen.

▲ *These wrestlers are from an inscription in the Temple of Ramses III in Egypt, which dates back to 1186 B.C. Before each bout, the wrestlers would rub oil over their bodies to make it difficult for their opponent to grip them. The figure on the left is about to be thrown.*

WRESTLING

Wrestling is the oldest and most widely distributed sport in the world. Some of the earliest references to wrestling can be found in ancient Egyptian art. An Egyptian tomb fresco gives a view of what wrestling was like about 4,000 years ago. Two figures, one painted brown and the other red, demonstrate over 120 different wrestling holds and throws. The sport was taken very seriously and it was professional then, just as it is today. Placards were carried with pictures of wrestling men on them. They represented the wrestlers' profession like a badge. Wrestling was also the most popular sport among the ancient Greeks. It is watched on television all over the world today.

FENCING

Besides wrestling, the ancient Egyptians enjoyed other competitive sports that involved fighting. One ancient

Egyptian sport was a kind of fencing with sticks rather than swords. The stick was held in the right hand, while the left hand held a shield for protection. Some competitors wore helmets to protect their heads and faces. Sometimes mock battles took place with large numbers of fighters on both sides. One tomb fresco, dating from about 1160 B.C., shows a stick fight between Egyptians, black Africans, and a fighter from the Middle East. This may be the first recorded example of international competition. Ancient Egyptian team games included the "Tug of War," which is still a popular game in many countries today. Alongside the pictures of these battles, there are comments such as "My team is stronger than yours" and orders such as "Hold fast, comrades."

▲ The crews of these papyrus rafts are mock fighting on their return from a hunting expedition. You can see the birds they have caught in a box. The boats are made of bundles of reeds tied together.

◄ Modern fencing is so fast that the fencers have to wear pads wired for electronic scoring. Hits are registered by a noise.

▼ *In this banquet from around 1550 B.C., the food is piled high in a colorful display on the right, while two young girls dance to the music of the double flute.*

MUSIC

Music is heard everywhere today. At weddings, happy music celebrates a marriage; workers often play light music in factories and workshops to help them work; and dance clubs play music you can dance to. Music was used in a similar way by the ancient Egyptians, who were great lovers of music, particularly of strong rhythms.

The rich and leisured Egyptians demanded music throughout the day, especially during meals. A typical orchestra consisted of two flute players, two harpists, singers, and clappers (people who clapped rhythmically with the music).During huge religious or royal events, larger numbers of musicians were used. Women clappers, pipers, and singers entertained farmers working in the fields and fishermen catching fish in the rivers. Music helped relieve the boredom of long hours of work. The rhythm might have also helped teams work well together; for example, helping fishermen pull in their nets in time with one another.

CHILDREN'S GAMES

Egyptian children in ancient times played speed and agility games just like those played in school playgrounds today. One was a high-jump game in which one child leaped over the joined feet and fingers of two others. In another game a child knelt on the ground with one leg stretched out. The other players had to touch the child with their feet without being touched themselves. Whoever was caught had to take over on the ground. Evidence from Egyptian tombs and graves shows that ball games were also played. Some balls – which have been preserved and found today – were made of seamed, colored leather, packed with straw or reeds. Other balls were wooden, like the ones used in carnival games such as Skeeball.

▲ **The origins of the harp**
Harps originated in ancient Egypt and came in all shapes and sizes. Many were hand-held, but others were played while kneeling. Some were as tall as the player and were played standing up. Egyptian harps had up to twenty strings.

▶ *The marshes of the Nile contained many species of waterfowl, such as herons, geese, and cormorants, which were hunted by the ancient Egyptians. This hunter, standing firmly in his boat, is about to launch a "throw-stick" at birds as they take off.*

HUNTING

Today, hunting takes place in many countries, although it is not as popular a form of entertainment as it used to be. Modern hunting includes shooting game or clay pigeons with high-velocity rifles or shotguns. Before 5000 B.C., hunting was an essential way of obtaining food. However, as societies gradually became based on farming, hunting also became a means of military training and a chance for leaders to impress their subjects. In ancient Egypt, pharaohs roamed the plains of the Upper Nile in their war chariots in search of big game such as elephants, rhinoceroses, cattle, and crocodiles. Their weapons were bows and arrows, lassos, spears, and bolas (ropes that had a stone attached to each end). When thrown at an animal, the bola wrapped itself around the animal's legs and slowed it or brought it down. Ancient bolas are very similar to the bolas used to bring down cattle on the plains of South America today.

Pharaohs liked their peasants to see them hunting hippopotamuses. The hippos could wreak havoc on crops around the Nile, and the peasants, who were not allowed to carry weapons, could do nothing about them. By keeping the number of hippos down, the pharaohs kept their popularity among their subjects and were considered worthy kings and leaders.

▲ *These hunters are looking for hippopotamuses in a papyrus swamp while a crocodile lurks under their raft.*

◄ *Modern hunting, with high-velocity rifles, is often just for entertainment. Pheasants, for example, are bred especially to be shot in the hunting season.*

▲ *These Greek theater masks are copies of the original ancient masks. They have real hair attached to them and holes for the eyes and mouth.*

chapter five

ANCIENT GREECE

If you go to a play at the theater, you may notice two masks on the program. These are used as symbols for drama societies or film companies. One mask is happy, the other sad. These masks were used by the ancient Greeks in their plays, in a civilization which was at its peak between 800 – 331 B.C. Masks were important in ancient Greek theater for a number of reasons. They helped the audience to identify the characters easily. Since all the actors were male, they helped male actors to play female parts in a simple disguise. The masks also acted as loudspeakers, because the shape of the mouth helped sounds to travel much farther. Finally, the expressions on the masks made it very clear to the audience how the characters were feeling.

Today's television includes situation comedies, thrillers, and soap operas. Some make you laugh, some are exciting, and some make you sad. Ancient Greek theater also produced a variety of plays. They were comedies, tragedies, or satyr plays. Tragedies were serious plays and had sad endings. They often dealt with events drawn from myths, such as the terrible things that happened to the soldiers in the legendary

◄ *This is a modern performance of the Greek tragedy,* Oedipus Rex. *In the play, Oedipus, who is abandoned by his parents as a baby, grows up, kills his father, and marries his mother without knowing it. When he finds out, he blinds himself and his mother kills herself.*

Trojan Wars of the twelfth century B.C. Masks in these plays would look sad or tortured. Comedies, however, were full of jokes and had happy endings, while satyr plays poked fun at serious topics. The masks in these plays were often smiling. The Greek comic dramatist Aristophanes cleverly made fun of situations in everyday life, politicians, or even the gods.

Modern theater has inherited words from ancient Greek theater. For example, the actors' changing room behind the orchestra was called a "skene," which is where the modern word "scene" comes from. Ancient Greek plays are often revived on modern stages. Aristophanes' play, *Lysistrata*, for example, was first performed in 411 B.C., but it contains many modern ideas. It concerns a group of women who try to prevent a war by stopping their husbands from fighting. The play's message of peace is very topical in the modern age. The play also seems modern in its positive portrayal of women taking control of their lives and making decisions for themselves.

▼ *A statue of a Greek comic actor impersonating a slave.*

OLYMPIC GAMES

Greece was the home of the original Olympics, which took place in 776 B.C. The ancient Olympic Games were used by each Greek state to show off its wealth and status in competition with rival states. The athletes' training was also seen as a good preparation for war. Similar political rivalry between states is very common today. In 1980, when the Olympic Games were held in the former Soviet Union, the Russians tried to show their country in a good light. However, the United States and a number of other countries boycotted the Moscow Olympics as a protest against the Soviet Union's invasion of Afghanistan.

▼ *The Los Angeles Olympics in 1984 used Sam the Eagle as the mascot of the Games, because the eagle is the symbol of the United States.*

▲ *In the 1988 Olympics in Seoul, South Korea, Ben Johnson appeared to have won the 100 meter race. He was later stripped of his title, however, because he had cheated and had used drugs to help him win. Some ancient Greek Olympians also tried to win by cheating.*

One of the most popular ancient events would never be allowed in the modern Olympics. The "Pankration" event, from the Greek word meaning "all-powerful," was a combination of wrestling, boxing, and judo, but there were few rules and regulations. The fighters punched, elbowed, kicked, kneed, and head-butted each other. The only form of aggression not allowed was biting and gouging out of each other's eyes. Evidence shows that this was the most popular event!

Four years later, when the Olympics were held in Los Angeles, the Soviet Union and its allied countries boycotted the Games. The United States used the Olympics to show America off, and the opening ceremony was similar to a huge Hollywood musical. In the modern Olympic Games, the competition among countries trying to appear better than other countries is very similar to that in the ancient Olympics.

Even in the ancient Olympics, heavy fines were imposed on athletes for bribery, cheating, and lying. One athlete was fined for lying to the judges. He said he was late arriving at the Games because his ship had been delayed by bad weather, but witnesses saw him at another games, winning prize money.

Dead Winner
In one Pankration event, the champion Arrachion died from strangulation just at the moment his opponent surrendered. The judges still crowned the dead Arrachion with the wreath and proclaimed him the winner.

Sunstroke
Spectators at the ancient Olympic Games had to watch the events with bare heads, out of respect for their gods. As the Games were held in the summer, many spectators suffered from sunstroke. The famous scientist and astronomer Thales died of sunstroke at the Games.

▼ *These long-distance runners are on an ancient Greek vase, dating back to 470 B.C. They are just about to go around the turning post on the left.*

The fines collected from athletes paid for statues around the Olympic site, which served as a warning to cheats. Athletes who appeared in the Olympic Games also traveled to other games, where they could win cash prizes. When an athlete brought great fame to his home town, he was sometimes granted free meals for life. Today's athletes compete all over the world and are sometimes paid generous appearance money or win television advertising contracts.

At first, the ancient Olympic Games lasted only one day, and consisted only of running races; other events were introduced later. The athletes had to compete completely naked and barefoot. This rule was later applied to the trainers of the athletes as well, after an incident concerning

an athlete's mother. Women were not allowed as spectators at the games. A woman who wanted to see her son compete in the boxing event disguised herself as a man and pretended to be her son's trainer. When her son won, she leaped over a barrier in her excitement and, when her disguise fell off, gave herself away. After this, a rule was established that all trainers must go as naked as the athletes.

▶ Sports Centers

The ancient Greeks were building sports centers by the third century B.C. The Great Gymnasium and Palaestra (athletics hall) in Olympia provided a covered running track and wrestling ground where Olympic athletes could train in bad weather.

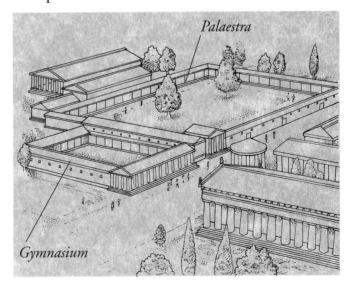

Palaestra

Gymnasium

▶ *These clay models show two ladies playing the game Pentalitha, or knucklebones. They are holding the joints of animal bones, which were the game pieces. The game of chance depended on how the bones landed after they were thrown.*

▼ *Roulette is a modern game that depends on chance, just like the ancient Greek game of Pentalitha. In roulette, players bet on where the ball will land after the ball is dropped into the spinning roulette wheel.*

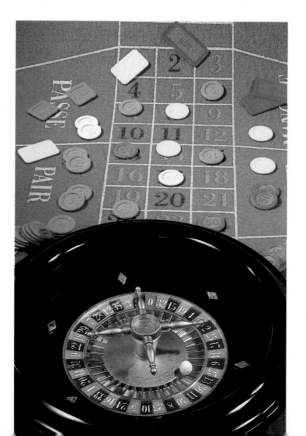

INDOOR GAMES

Apart from the great Olympic event, there were other entertainments, especially for children and wealthy women. In the modern game of Jacks, angular pieces of metal have to be picked up in the time it takes for a ball to bounce. The game originated from the ancient Greek game called Pentalitha, meaning knucklebones, because the original pieces used were the joints of animal bones. Kollabismos was a Greek version of the modern Blind Man's Bluff. A blindfolded player was smacked by another player and had to find out who it was. Askoliasmos was a messier version of the modern game Twister, where the players had to stand and balance on a wineskin covered with olive oil. Children's toys found in ancient Greek tombs consist of small clay figures riding horses and other animals. They are not so different from the plastic or metal figures for children today.

MUSIC

Music and song were important in Greek birth, marriage, and funeral ceremonies, just as they are to modern ceremonies. Instruments such as the lyre, harp, flute, and panpipes were played. All the events at the Olympic Games – aside from running – were accompanied by pipe and flute playing.

◄ *This ancient Greek vase shows Terpsichore, the goddess of dance and song, playing the harp. She is flanked by women playing the double flute and the lyre. Although hardly any ancient Greek music has survived, we know that it was central to everyday life. Even Greek hoplites (warriors) were accompanied by flute playing as they advanced into battle.*

chapter six

ANCIENT ROME

The great spectator sports of the modern world thrive on big occasions such as the Super Bowl, the World Series, and the World Cup. During these events, huge stadia containing over 100,000 people each are packed with spectators, and the events are televised all over the world. The ancient Romans built the first stadia between c.507 B.C. and A.D. 476 for their contests, races, and games. They were so obsessed by their games that it was said that the citizens of Rome were interested only in entertainment and food. In Rome itself, two huge monuments to entertainment were built: the Colosseum, which held 50,000 people, for gladiatorial contests, and the Circus Maximus, a specially designed course for chariot racing, which held 200,000 people.

In the 1990s, the television game show *American Gladiators* brought gladiators into modern entertainment. In the game show, modern gladiators took part in physical contests with members of the public. Of course, on this program and similar ones no one fights actually to the death!

▲ *In this model of Imperial Rome, you can see the circular Colosseum in the center and the oval-shaped Circus Maximus in the foreground. The island in the middle of the Circus Maximus was known as the "Spina" and the charioteers had to race around this in a counter-clockwise direction.*

The beginnings of the gladitorial contests are thought to go back to the Etruscans, a people of northern Italy who were absorbed into the Roman empire. Roman gladiators were extremely popular fighters. At first, slaves were ordered to fight and passers-by were charged to watch and take a seat. This was how the gladiatorial contest was born. The gladiators were slaves who went to special training schools to be taught the art of fighting. Roman audiences loved to see fights between different types of gladiators. Some were armed with short swords and small shields, while others fought with a spear and a net. If a gladiator's performance had not pleased the spectators, they would condemn him to death. Some gladiators survived many fights, became famous, and bought their freedom.

▲ *These modern "gladiators" are only mock fighting in this television game show, using plastic hammers instead of swords. Like their Roman predecessors, they wear protective helmets.*

▲ *These Roman gladiators are fighting to the death with swords in a test of strength and skill.*

Mad Caligula
The games were used by the Romans to execute enemies and criminals. However, during Emperor Caligula's reign (A.D. 37– 41), he was so angry when there were no prisoners to kill that he decided to throw a crowd of spectators into the arena to be slaughtered by wild beasts.

▶ *These soldiers are killing leopards for the entertainment of an important Roman called Magerius. The soldiers are paid 1,000 denarii each for this, which Magerius' servant brings out in bags on a tray.*

▲ *Bullfighting in Spain is a controversial blood sport today, just as it was in Roman times. The bull, weakened by the banderillas in his neck, is about to be killed by a matador with a sword, just visible under the red cape.*

BLOOD SPORTS

Animals were brought from all over the Roman Empire to fight with gladiators in specially built arenas called amphitheaters. Hundreds of thousands of animals were killed in this way. The great orator Cicero wrote about his reaction to such blood sports to a friend: "…what pleasure can it possibly be to a man of culture whether a human being is ripped apart by a powerful beast, or a splendid beast is killed with a spear." Cicero was in the minority in this opinion, however; most of the ancient Romans enjoyed such events.

RATINGS

Just as public viewership is important to television networks today, popularity was important in the Roman games. New and impressive spectacles had to be displayed to attract people. Sometimes an aqueduct was fed into the amphitheater so that sea-battles could be reenacted.

Spectators at the Games watch what are probably prisoners being fed to wild animals.

▶ *This four-horse chariot is approaching the three columns of the turning post. Chariot races were a mass of confusion, dust and noise. The course was seven laps of the track, and on each day there could be as many as twenty races.*

Sports mad
Nero (A.D. 54–68) was so fanatical about the chariot races that when his wife Poppaea complained about his late return from them, he murdered her!

RACING

Throughout history, people have wanted to drive their vehicles as fast as possible. The fastest four-wheeled vehicles today can be seen on the Indy Car and Grand Prix circuits. You can often see the winners wearing laurel wreaths while spraying their huge bottles of champagne, and some auto racing teams and tire companies use the laurel wreath in their advertising. The laurel wreath is a legacy from Greek and Roman times, when wreaths were awarded to the champions of chariot races. Chariot racing was very popular among the Greeks, and the Romans made it into a favorite mass-spectator sport. As in the Indy Car and Grand Prix circuits, the charioteers formed teams, known as factions: Blue, Green, White, and Red. Sometimes different colors were associated with different political or religious groups. The charioteers were often slaves or from the poorer classes, but if they won they could become very famous. They could then go to the faction that offered them the greatest amount of money. Chariot racing was a very dangerous sport. During the high-speed races, the charioteer tried to smash his chariot into his opponent's, hoping to destroy it. This was known as shipwrecking, and the "wrecked" charioteer had to cut the reins or be violently dragged to certain death. Today, the sport of harness racing is a nonviolent version of Roman chariot racing. In harness racing, single horses pull two-wheeled carts in a race around a track. The horse can only trot because the chariot is attached very closely behind, whereas in ancient Roman chariot racing, four horses were able to gallop freely.

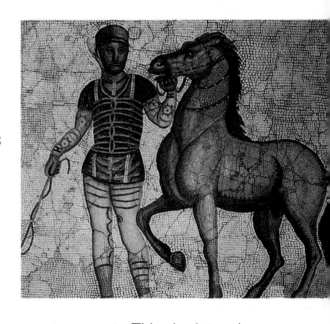

▲ *This charioteer is wearing the racing colors of his sponsor, just as racing jockeys today wear the colors of their horse owners. He wears a protective leather helmet. Modern jockeys wear harder helmets called skull caps.*

RIOTING

Rioting, or hooliganism, is often thought to be the result of modern times, particularly surrounding soccer. However, violence among team supporters dates right back to the followers of ancient chariot factions. Supporters for the Blues and the Greens were fanatical. Followers were obsessed by their favorite drivers and their color. In the eastern Roman Empire's capital, Constantinople, rioting fans burned down the wooden arena for chariot racing five times before the emperor replaced it with a stone one. The worst riot was in A.D. 532, when the Green and Blue factions rioted. The army was called in and an estimated 30,000 people were killed.

◄ *Modern harness racing is the nearest we have to chariot racing today. Harness racing is very popular in the United States, Australia, and many countries in Europe.*

HEALTH CLUBS

Health clubs are very popular in modern times. They are used for activities such as swimming, racquetball, and weight-lifting, and for saunas, and jacuzzis. More than 2,000 years ago, the Roman baths provided similar facilities. Roman towns and cities had at least one public bath, which provided many attractions other than bathing. Baths were important meeting places and often became the social center of the town. Apart from bathing, the baths

Bath Times
The Romans were very tolerant and allowed mixed bathing at first, but Emperor Hadrian (A.D. 117 – 138) thought it immoral and passed a law forbidding it. After this, women bathed during the morning and men bathed during the afternoon and evening.

▶ *The Roman Baths in Bath, England, are well-preserved. Special underground heating systems called "hypocausts" made bathers sweat. Once the sweat was wiped off, bathers took hot or cold plunge baths.*

Large indoor swimming pools, like this water park in Alberta, Canada, are popular places to spend leisure time, just as the bath houses were in the Roman Empire.

provided gyms, bowling alleys, wine bars, snack bars, and reading rooms. It was quite common to work out in the gym, clean up in a bath, and enjoy a glass of wine with a snack. The baths were highly organized, and the larger ones could accommodate thousands of people. They were reasonably priced so that most people could afford them.

Romans relaxed in bars like this one, from A.D. 100 in Ostia, Italy. Ostia was the port for Rome.

chapter seven

ANCIENT CHINA

HORSES

Horses today are used in many sports and entertainments including polo, racing, and show jumping. Polo, which originated in Persia, was being played in China by the seventh century A.D. Like the game today, two teams of riders used their mallets to try to hit a wooden ball through their opponents' goal posts. Sometimes the game was more like a target practice than a competition between teams. Their mallets resembled the clubs used by hunters on

Badminton
The ancient Chinese may have invented badminton. There are ancient records that describe a missile made of a lightweight copper cone with feathers inserted into it – the first shuttlecock.

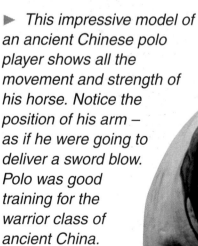
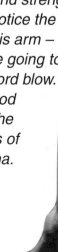

▶ *This impressive model of an ancient Chinese polo player shows all the movement and strength of his horse. Notice the position of his arm – as if he were going to deliver a sword blow. Polo was good training for the warrior class of ancient China.*

◀ Modern polo can be fast and dangerous for both the rider and the horse.

horseback. The game required expert horse riding and it became a fashionable sport played by both men and women. Since horses were expensive to keep and train, just as they are today, the sport was played mainly by royalty and the rich.

▼ This modern golfer is playing a game that could be more than 2,000 years old.

GOLF

Golf is another popular modern sport, with new golf courses opening frequently. Golf tournaments, such as the American Masters, have huge followings and are given extensive television coverage. In China, a form of golf called *Wan-Chin* was being played by the sixth century A.D. A manual written in that century explains the rules of *Wan-Chin*, describing the ball, clubs, fouls, number of players, and conditions of the course. The manual warns that the game was suitable only for gentlemen, which was also the early attitude of British golfers. Many ancient Chinese officials and politicians found the game so enjoyable that they disregarded their public duties in order to play.

Yin and Yang
The Yin and Yang
that the poet Lu Yu
referred to is a
traditional belief of
the Chinese. They
believed that forces
should perfectly
balance each other.
Yang represents light,
summer, and warmth,
while Yin represents
darkness, winter,
and cold.

SOCCER

One of the most popular sports in the world is soccer. The earliest evidence of a game resembling soccer is in China. The game, played in northern China from at least the third century B.C., did not allow players to use their arms, so that their feet would keep warm. The game was referred to as *tsu chu*, *tsu* meaning "to kick with the foot," and *chu* meaning "the stuffed leather ball." There was even poetry written about *tsu chu*. The poet Lu Yu (A.D. 1125– 1210) hung his poetry on the goal posts, similar to the banners that fans bring to sporting events today, showing support for their favorite teams and players. Here is one of Yu's ancient poems:

> *A round ball and a square goal*
> *suggest the shape of Yin and the Yang.*
> *The ball is like the full moon*
> *and the two teams stand opposed;*
> *captains are appointed and take their place*

Yu's words show how seriously the Chinese took the game:

> *Determination and coolness are essential*
> *and there must not be the slightest irritation for failure.*
> *Such is the game. Let its principles apply to life.*

▶ *Banners and flags are an important part of the sporting tradition. These Brazilian fans, whose team has just won the 1970 World Cup held in Mexico, support their team with banners, drums, and smoke bombs.*

◄ *Archery is a legacy from ancient China. The Chinese developed the composite bow between A.D. 400–500. These first bows were made of thin strips of wood that were laminated with animal sinew, giving them double the tension and fire-power of ordinary bows of a similar weight.*

▼ **Wrestling**
Like the Egyptians, the ancient Chinese were wrestling over 2,000 years ago. This bronze statuette is from between the fourth and the third centuries B.C.

ARCHERY

Archery is gaining popularity today, with thousands of participants around the world. Modern bows are high-tech machines, made with complicated sights and balances. In ancient China, archery was of great importance to warriors. Chinese warriors practiced constantly, trying to pierce fabric and metal with specially prepared, heavy arrows. Archery was used by the peasantry to hunt for food to supplement their diet. The upper classes held exclusive competitions where the participants, all beautifully dressed and on horseback, fired one arrow in front of, one behind, and one from the side of a charging horse.

THEATER AND FESTIVALS

Chinese theater started in ancient times as a mobile tradition of acrobatics and song. Chinese circus and opera troupes traveled from city to city to put on their performances, a tradition popular with the emperors of China. Performers jumped, tumbled, and juggled with tables, ropes, hoops, balls, clubs, and knives, entertaining people in streets and marketplaces. Modern Chinese circuses are still famous for their acrobats and jugglers. Ancient Chinese troupes were invited to festivals related to the lunar calendar. These festivals included the New Year

▶ *Chinese festivals are still celebrated according to the lunar calendar today, especially by Chinese communities living in Western cities, such as the Chinatowns of Vancouver in Canada, San Francisco in California, and London in England. Like the theater, Chinese festivals use exotic costumes and makeup.*

◀ *This Chinese opera, performed in Penang, Malaysia, uses brilliant scenery and extravagant costume.*

and Midsummer festivals, and those of the August and September moons, which celebrated the harvest and selling of crops. In these festivals, which are still celebrated today, villages and towns competed to hire the most famous and expensive troupes. This still happens among towns in modern arts festivals today. Ancient Chinese theater is famous for its exotic costumes, bright makeup, and loud music. The makeup, like the masks in ancient Greek theater, made it easy for the audience to recognize characters. The makeup also helped the male actors play female parts because, as in Greek theater, women were not allowed on the stage. Gongs, kettledrums, and numerous wind instruments interrupted the actors' voices, and the audiences responded loudly to jokes, just like modern audiences attending the taping of television situation comedies, or the audiences of stand-up comedians.

▼ *The ancient Chinese discovered gunpowder and created spectacular fireworks. Modern cities often celebrate special occasions with a fireworks display, such as this one on Sydney Harbor in Australia on New Year's Eve.*

Ancient Greece and Crete

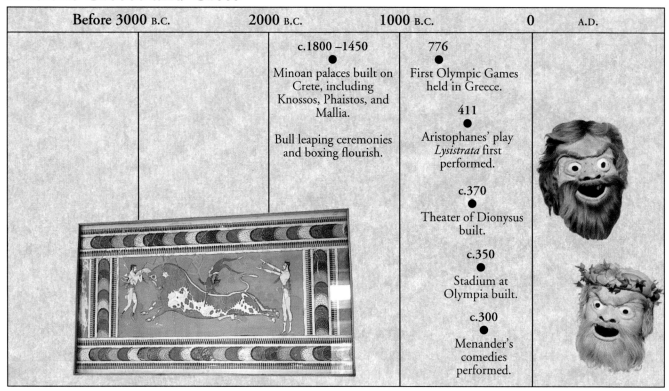

Before 3000 B.C.	2000 B.C.	1000 B.C.	0	A.D.

c.1800–1450

Minoan palaces built on Crete, including Knossos, Phaistos, and Mallia.

Bull leaping ceremonies and boxing flourish.

776

First Olympic Games held in Greece.

411

Aristophanes' play *Lysistrata* first performed.

c.370

Theater of Dionysus built.

c.350

Stadium at Olympia built.

c.300

Menander's comedies performed.

Ancient Rome

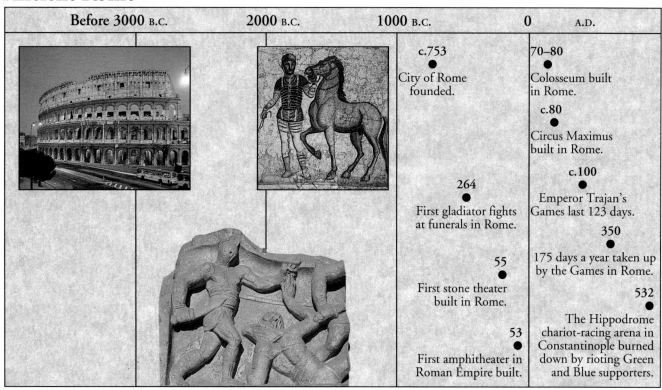

Before 3000 B.C.	2000 B.C.	1000 B.C.	0	A.D.

c.753

City of Rome founded.

264

First gladiator fights at funerals in Rome.

55

First stone theater built in Rome.

53

First amphitheater in Roman Empire built.

70–80

Colosseum built in Rome.

c.80

Circus Maximus built in Rome.

c.100

Emperor Trajan's Games last 123 days.

350

175 days a year taken up by the Games in Rome.

532

The Hippodrome chariot-racing arena in Constantinople burned down by rioting Green and Blue supporters.

Ancient China

Before 3000 b.c.	2000 b.c.	1000 b.c.	0	A.D.

c.2500
Central Asian people tame horses.

631
Boxing practiced.

c.500
Wrestling. practiced.

221–210
First empire in China ruled by Emperor Ch'in.

c.100
Soccer called "tsu chu" played.

c.200
Polo invented in Persia.

c.200–300
Early form of badminton played.

c.500
Early form of golf played, called "Wan-Chin."

c. 600
Polo played in China as a sport and for military training.

1125–1210
Poetry about football written by Lu Yu.

Ancient Egypt

Before 3000 B.C.	2000 B.C.	1000 B.C.	0	A.D.

3100
Egyptian civilization flourishes as the Upper and Lower kingdoms are joined.

2600
Great pyramid built, Giza.

c.2100
Wrestling practiced.

c.1900
Wine-making and drinking are popular.

1640
Last pyramids built.

1333–1323
Pharaoh Tutankhamun hunts lions from a chariot.

c. 1160
Stick fighting played.

c.800
A cult is centered around the cat goddess Bastet, who is the patron of music and dancing.

450
Egyptian stick fighting described as part of a cult ceremony by the writer Herodotus.

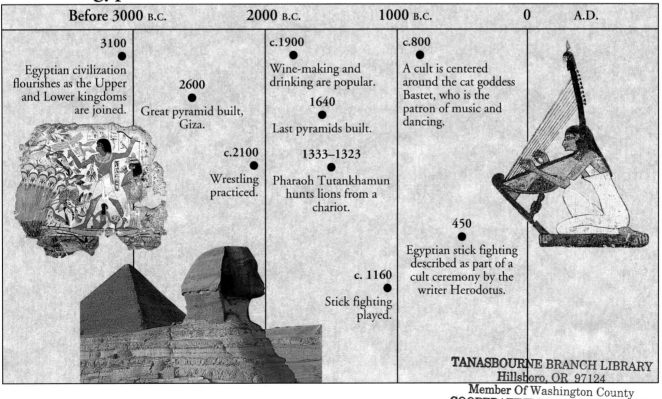

45

GLOSSARY

Aqueduct   A bridge for carrying water above ground.

Blood sports   Sports that involve killing.

Boycotted   Deliberately avoided.

Bribery   The giving or taking of secret gifts with the knowledge of getting something dishonestly or illegally.

Chariot   An open, two-wheeled vehicle pulled by horses.

Charioteers   Chariot drivers.

Developed countries   Countries that have a high standard of living based on industry and trade.

Fanatical   Feeling excessively strong about something.

Fertility   The ability of land to produce seeds or plants or of animals to reproduce.

Frescoes   Paintings made on walls covered with fresh, damp plaster.

Gladiators   Men, usually slaves, who were specially trained to fight to the death in Roman public arenas.

Hollywood   An area in Los Angeles, in California, where the movie industry was based; also used to mean the movie industry.

Lassoed   Caught by means of a long rope with a loop at the end.

Laurel wreaths   The leaves of a laurel shrub made into a garland, usually in a ring shape.

Leisure time   Free time when people are not working.

Mallets   Wooden hammers.

Myths   Made-up stories about heroes or gods of ancient times.

Nobility   Nobles – people of high rank in a country.

Pharaoh   An Egyptian king.

Political intrigue   In government, the scheming of people to get advantage over others.

Rodeo   A competitive sport, usually in North America, where cowboys display their skills: bareback riding, roping cattle, bull riding, etc.

Stone Age   The period before 6000 B.C. when stone was used for tools and weapons.

Stadia   Large, open-air sports grounds with rows of seats for spectators to watch events.

Thongs   Strips of leather, which are used for fastening.

Trojan Wars   Legendary conflicts between Greece and the city of Troy, in what is today known as Turkcy.

Waterfowl   Birds that live on or near the water.

FURTHER READING

Barrett, Norman. *Sport: Players, Games & Spectacle.* Timelines. New York: Franklin Watts, 1993.

Barrett, Norman. *The World Cup.* New York: Thomson Learning, 1994.

Clare, John D., ed. *Classical Rome.* Living History. San Diego: Harcourt Brace, 1993.

Glubock, Shirley and Tamarin, Alfred. *The Olympic Games in Ancient Greece.* New York: HarperCollins Children's Books, 1976.

Odijk, Pamela. *The Egyptians.* The Ancient World. Morristown, NJ: Silver Burdett, 1989.

Pryor, Nick. *Putting on a Play.* New York: Thomson Learning, 1994.

Santrey, Laurence. *Music.* Keeping in Touch Library. Mahwah, NJ: Troll Books, 1985.

Waterlow, Julia. *The Ancient Chinese.* Look Into the Past. New York: Thomson Learning, 1994.

Picture acknowledgments:
The publishers would like to thank the following for allowing their pictures to be used in this book:
Action Plus 13 (top); All-Sport (U.K.) Ltd. 24 (top & bottom); Ancient Art & Architecture Collection 12, 22, 44 (top right); C M Dixon 7, 13 (bottom), 21 (top), 23 (top & bottom), 28 (top), 30, 31 (bottom), 32 (top), 33, 35 (top), 37 (bottom), 41 (bottom), 44 (bottom & middle), 45 (top right); Eye Ubiquitous 11 (bottom), 35 (bottom), 42, 43 (bottom); Sonia Halliday 4, 10, 44 (top left); Robert Harding 4, 8-9, 11 (top), 32 (bottom), 36; Images Colour Library 6-7; London Weekend Television 31 (top); Michael Holford *Cover (inset),* 14, 20, 25, 26, 29, 34, 45 (bottom left); Tony Stone Worldwide *Cover (main),* 5, 15, 17 (bottom), 37 (top), 39 (top & bottom), 40, 41 (top), 44 (bottom left); Wayland Picture Library 43 (top); Werner Forman Archive 4, 5, 16, 17 (top), 18, 19, 38, 44 (top left & bottom right); Zefa 9, 21 (bottom), 27, 28 (bottom).
All artwork is by Peter Bull.

INDEX

Numbers in **bold** refer to illustrations.